THE NATURE OF THE MOMENT

By the same Author
★
WHETHER A DOVE OR SEAGULL
(*with Sylvia Townsend Warner*)

THE NATURE OF THE MOMENT

By
Valentine Ackland

A NEW DIRECTIONS BOOK

Copyright © Sylvia Townsend Warner 1973
Library of Congress Catalog Card Number: 73-84871
All rights reserved. Except for brief
passages quoted in a newspaper, magazine,
radio, or television review, no part
of this book may be reproduced in any form
or by any means, electronic or mechanical,
including photocopying and recording,
or by any information storage and retrieval system,
without permission in writing from the Publisher.

ISBN 978-0-8112-1818-4 ISBN 0-8112-1818-X

New Directions Books
are published for James Laughlin
by New Directions Publishing Corporation,
333 Sixth Avenue, New York 10014

Printed in Great Britain by
T. H. Brickell & Son Ltd.
The Blackmore Press, Gillingham, Dorset

CONTENTS

The winter woods	page 9
I sit here writing	9
Wrist-bound, the falcon	10
The rocket is loosed	10
POET	11
How lose the red wine	12
Space is invisible waves	12
From the far past	13
SUMMER STORM	13
FANNY BRAWNE'S LETTER	13
Built out of dark shapes	14
Plato would have listened	15
When I have said	15
Where you will go	16
Ponder the world upon	16
POEM IN 1936	17
POEM IN 1938	17
PROPHETIC POEM	18
GREEK, THE WORLD'S TONGUE	19
DEDICATION SET OVER A CRATER, 1941	21
Slowly over the beautiful spaces	21
From WAR IN PROGRESS:	
1 March, 1940	22
6 August, 1940	23
7 October, 1940	24
Black-Out	25
Notes on Life at Home, February, 1942	25
THE NATURE OF THE MOMENT	26
TEACHING TO SHOOT	27
READING MY OWN WORKS	27
In those far mornings	28
NEW PAULUS SILENTIARIUS	29
SALTHOUSE, NEW YEAR'S EVE	30

The white tread of the poet	page 31
IMPRESSION OF THOUGHT	31
IN DREAMS, IN VISIONS OF THE NIGHT	32
The daggers dreamed	33
ROUSSEAU'S PICTURE: 'THE FOREST'	33
Every day perhaps	34
DREAM	34
The honey-pale lioness	35
DREAM LANDSCAPE WITH GIRL	35
The long future	36
The rich horn	36
From where we walk	37
Do you ever look over	37
JOURNEY FROM WINTER	39
OF DEATH AND JUDGEMENT	40
NOTES FROM A DIARY	41
Does the lark	42
On this day	42
I walked through a wood	43
In time ago	43
All those who stray	44
The white face of the Moon	44
The guiltless Ape	45
The silence develops after	45
I stared through the opening	46
Like the dearest child	46
Watch the round drop	46
The most persuasive argument	47
Whether the lost thing found	47
IN THE BEGINNING	48
The cuckoo sang	49
The skull leaned forward	49
A MOMENT OF TIME	50
I saw my shadow	50

ON LAYING DOWN MY PEN	*page* 51
This early morning	52
I remember the story	52
ON A WINTER JOURNEY	53
There were times long ago	54
POEM FOR THE PASSING OF POETRY	54
AUTOBIOGRAPHICAL	55
Where there is something	56
The sea-crab swings	56
HOPE OF POETRY	57
Into this brief and angry place	58
For all that takes place	59
Lead, somehow	59
VARIATIONS ON A THEME:	
1934	59
1936	60
1943	61
1948	61
1950	61
1957	62

The winter woods against this yellow sky
Stand like embroidered trees
Worked in memorial hair;

So still against the clouds the branches lie,
Drooping as if to please
The grief that placed them there.

The stable cistern, like a funeral urn,
Outlined in strong relief
Stands up beneath the boughs;

As if with evening nature would return
To mourn some ancient grief
No younger heart allows.

I sit here writing in the middle hour of night;
All's quiet and has been for some hours before
I hear a slight sound out beyond the door—
A crying sound, but very brief and slight.

So I get up from the table, and stand to hear,
And it is there again. Opening the door I see
The kitten outside, who has made this call to me,
Frightened of the dark passage, stiff with fear—

I sit at the table again and write this down;
He squats in front of the fire and blinks his eyes;
I consider God again, join with the hopeless wise
In thinking him harsh, who shuts us out, if indeed he has known.

Wrist-bound, the falcon goes
Most freely; tethered here
And hooded, leather-blinded,
But through brown feathers the wind blows.

Unhampered he by fears;
Free, were he minded,
To fret against the sky—
But tense he waits and set he hears

Silence; till sound sings
A whistle in his ears:
Hood gone, wrist lifts and throws
Him clean. As the air veers, he springs.

The rocket is loosed—the last, and let off late—
And winds in a flash its sky-way;
But, ah! not straight, not forging straight—
Writhing to heaven, not piercing, and heaven is high,

Heaven is dark and away.
Not stoop, the sky, will never stoop down to meet
Brief twine of flame, this must fall to ground and die,
As we—but no, so much more fierce and fleet,

Yet fallen, fallen as we,
To darkness and earth and silence. The unpierced sky
Not touched by even that sharp and well-aimed try—
Unmoved the night, and none to heed but I.

POET

As it cries out from under the cover
Of mind he rises up, leaves his lover,
Leaves his house, wealth, food behind
And goes out.

As it cries to him he answers, but obeys
Nothing he knows. Intermittently throughout his days
He follows, alone; scared when it shows,
Terrified when it dies to him.

And so on. He trembles when it calls him
But must follow. Suspicious of all that then befalls him
He loses peace, love, zest and finally life—
And nothing done.

And nothing done. For at the end all he masters
Is the route of the way of numberless disasters,
No more. And where all others have found their grief
He comes, too, to grief, alone.

How lose the red wine, lose the cuckoo's song,
Fresh white bread, or the glistening white of the may,
Blistering on the sky all a summer day,
All a summer day long?

How leave these things, I say—
While still the cuckoo sings, and others, strong
And light of foot, go up the hills, along
The green paths I trod on my summer day.
Why leave, I ask, when here where I belong
All is unchanged still, change me as I may—
Wine's red, bread's white, and ah! how white the may—

Space is invisible waves. In leaves of trees
Space-water rustles, and the sway of these
Is only movement of seaweed under tide,
In restless sway and swing from side to side—
While in the invisible air and in the sky
Spirits like deep-sea fishes are sweeping by.

And I on a hill-top in summer, when grass is brown,
Lying beneath the sky, and likely to drown
In the vast ocean of space passing to and fro . . .
Here, on the floor of the sea, starved thistles blow
And the wind is no wind but a fast-flowing current of tide,
And the spirits are blown and are driven, and cannot abide.

From the far past, from the far future, to this moment flows
Time, that bears the tiger and the frail, eternal rose;
Like a small star set in the vast firmament which holds
A million simultaneous fires shining between ice colds,
To Now, which is all we have, eternities deliver
Each one of us this present from the anonymous giver.
Choiceless, we must receive what's sent, the tiger and the rose,
The star's bright-burning life and death, and the immortal snows.

SUMMER STORM

'I will not!' I say, 'I will not!'—Saying
I will not, while all through the air around me
Resounds 'I will—I will!' Swallows playing,
Birdsong, leaved trees, all confound me—
Confuting truth with truth, hope against hope, despair
Bundled between them, by one side or the other
Used as a bludgeon—'I will not care—'
('I care—I care—I care—')

FANNY BRAWNE'S LETTER
PUT UNOPENED IN KEATS'S COFFIN

'Often, before I came to lie down here, I wept,
And over you—who lie here, silent and diminished,
The seal unbroken. Desire and sorrow long ago were finished;
Long ago now I came, lay down by you, and slept.'

Built out of dark shapes, green weight and corn-yellow,
  This midnight is a tall tower in my mind;
Trees are the hour, the height that round moon rising
  And thought, at last inaccurate, undefined,
Climbs up the steep, the tall tall tower,
  Leans out to see the deepening dark behind.

Not fear, not death; things more remote concern
This pondering thought now. Heavily through shadow
  Thought stares. Like chattering wheels the stars return
Unheeded; now Time's a tree soft-growing
  Darkly to darkness, and yellow as corn the heavy
Moon's height stands erect and seems to burn.

Owl's flight brushes a clean stroke of pallor
  Gently across thick green. Here held entranced
My quiet thought watches beauty and unchoosing
  Slides down, fast-following the momently glanced
Glory, and at once the structure dwindles
  Into its gentle dark. A midnight chanced

To build this refuge, while Time spun away
My treasure. Now the thought which leaned uncaring
  Has come to earth, slipped carelessly to clay
And brought the tall tower down. Now minutes falling
Drop through the midnight silence round as leaves—
  The bright moon falls as soundlessly as they.

Plato would have listened with pleasure to this country train,
Travelling noisily between the solemn hills,
Because the flurry and rattle is echoed so that an image
Unreal breathes into my right ear, while the transient fact
Of the train really passing roars into my left.
Philosophers enjoy such ratification of their notions
(Especially simple proofs of a gratifying complex fancy);
But people who are not philosophers and have only simple fancies
Rarely receive any ratifications at all.

When I have said 'I love you' I have said
Nothing at all to tell you; I cannot find
Any speech in any country of the mind
Which might inform you whither I have fled.
In saying 'I love you' I have gone so far
Away from you, into so strange a land;
You may not find me, may not understand
How I am exiled, driven to a star

Till now deserted. Here I stand about,
Eat, sleep, bewail, feel lonely and explore,
Remember how I loved the world, before,
Tremble in case that memory lets me out.
Islanded here, I wait for you to come—
Waiting the day that exiles you to home.

Where you will go—under the may-tree, round
The flaxen meadow, over the lawn grass—
Where you wander alone will be the sound,
Sweet as summer, of your dress as you pass.

Where the twigs catch it and thistles snatch it
And other fingers, fine, but not so shrewd as mine,
Your steps will lag and drag; your dress will tarry,
Listening—'Merry in summer to marry, to marry.'

Ponder the world upon; the shade and shine,
The flood and fall, increase and dwine,
The air, light and impersonal, over all,
Uncared, uncaring, obeying its rise and fall.

Seeing the world again, after the cold
Anger of night and day is over and told,
Mark how the level play, the steady tide,
Keeps fall and sway perpetually—Only man's pride

Can deny the law, can disobey,
Can dare, and does, say and unsay,
Promise and not fulfil, toss truth and lies,
Use as he pleases the meek earth and fettered skies.

POEM IN 1936

Only to you, my darling, to you only
in this world full of woe, in terror turning
both world and I lean love on this frail stay
of you, of your brief-burning summer day.

Nothing beyond, as all men know, but night:
afraid, but not to point of base believing
beyond clear truth, true love lays down his head
and goes to death as you and I to bed.

POEM IN 1938

How quickly the time goes,
how quickly, how quickly the time goes!
How loudly the storm blows,
how loudly, how loudly it blows!
Yet, talking of weather, we faithfully recall,
still faithfully recall,
the winter of twenty-eight when the pipes froze.

Ten years have gone,
ten years since then have gone:
time still marches on,
time and the weather still march on:
time and the weather and war, and still
we prefer to stay still,
ten years back it froze, and twenty a war was won.

PROPHETIC POEM

Down what river run the snows of last winter?
No wider now this water, although spring
Looks bright from hedge and meadow, and the sunshine
Warmly lays hands on head, makes everything
Melt from its winter cold, its fret and pine.

Down what river run the snows of last winter?
Heavy they lay, frozen like slabs of stone
Over the death that ill-sent season spread
Flat on the living; ah, and they died alone—
Those who are under the earth that lies on the dead.

Down what river run the snows of last winter?
They melted to water, and frozen grief to tears
Flowed down to the wide embrace of anonymous water;
They deepened the channel, this year and the other years,
To carry the flow of grief that is coming after:
Down all rivers will run the snows of next winter.

GREEK, THE WORLD'S TONGUE
(*On Rereading 'The Greek Anthology', 1941*)

I. REJECTED DEDICATION

To Pan, to Demeter, to sweet-voiced Apollo,
Long dedicate my flocks, my ploughlands were,
And, too, my orchard and my shady trees,
My smooth grass verges by the riverside;
But these old-fashioned offerings are mocked
And worthless found when all gods worship fire.

II. THE DEAD SAILOR

Thymodes' son was Lycus; mine no name
Needs now. He lies in nameless seas,
Drowned in an unnamed ship,
And even his last was but a dateless day.

III. SCHOLARS SLAIN

Whether a son survived to die of years,
Leaving thy grandsons, Heraclitus, so
To breed and die in ripeness, I know not;
But progeny, after prodigious time,
I find of thine. And they are ashes, too.

IV. OFFERINGS BEFORE BED

See, I have hung the coat, the shallow helmet,
And this untainted gas mask in the hall,
Placing shoes, torch, and the traveller's scrip nearby;
Thus, Lesbia, all is done that can be done,
Meet offering made, and no good spirit slighted;
Custom obeyed, let us upstairs to bed!

V. NEW MEN, NEW ART

Praxiteles wrung life from lifeless stone,
A godlike man. But later men than he,
Mighty as Zeus, send fire to kindle stone
And wring the heart of stone to murder life.

VI. DEDICATION

Androclus gave his bow, Apollo; I have only
This old, uncertain rifle, but I slew
Large game with it on a late summer day,
Winged game that tumbled helpless from the sky.

VII. SHRINE TO PALLAS ATHENE

Pallas, to honor the invincible
Bright arms you carry, we have made your shrine
Spacious in every country on the earth;
Broad fields with the ranged aircraft and vast graves
Deep in the groaning ground proclaim your glory.
Wisdom must wait her trophies till the end.

DEDICATION SET OVER A CRATER, 1941

Underneath the paving-stones
In a narrow refuge near the city drains,
My young wife in labour brought forth my daughter.

Bombs that screamed down from heaven
Were not portents of divine favour on the birth,
Foretold no noble fortune to the babe;
She lived to cry, to draw breath underground,
To open eyes on darkness and to hear death fall.

Persephone perhaps will weep to see
The mother's shade clasping that shadowy child—
But who will weep for me?

Slowly over the beautiful spaces
where no men are, slowly the dear sun rises
and day spreads long shadows at leisure, and gentle
all day the cool winds blow and no one is there.

All night over the solemn landscape
the moon moves and changes the outstretched shadows;
nothing breathes there but the silent, mysterious
breath of the plants in quietness and night.

From WAR IN PROGRESS
*A running commentary started in spring, 1941,
and continued till spring, 1943*

1 MARCH, 1940

Across the lovely skies of Spain
The Heinkels and Capronis came,
Over the houses of Madrid
The bombers flew as they were bid;
And none of this was as it seemed
We said, and we Non-Intervened.

Another note is struck just now:
England sets sail, Age at the prow;
The Heinkels (and Capronis too?)
Spin their propellers, start anew—
Foreigners are the first to suffer:
War's come, Non-Intervention over.

How hard the task of men who try
To find out when a man should die
And whether he, being justified
In dying, is happy to have died.

In Finland men for Mannerheim
Died, for the second and last time;
In England and in Germany
I die for Hans, Hans dies for me:
America remains the only
Country unslain, and feels quite lonely.

6 AUGUST, 1940

And now they've hit too hard. The trouble's started,
The finish is out of sight. The end has flown
Ahead to dig the graves and set the throne,
While hours and days combine to stretch the carpet—
   Blood-red in colour and more rich in pile
   Than you've seen yet, and richening all the while.

This is an epoch done, but who dares know it?
Force is become so mighty, nothing answers
Its loud remarks. Silence as flat as Flanders
Follows each shouted statement. We need a poet
   To answer it—or bigger bombers think you?
   Choose which you like, the answer's bound to sink you.

No peace now. In conformity with custom
Men will fight on till idiots only left
Creep to a thieves' den and condone the theft,
Blink at the murderers and agree to trust 'em
   And wait again. Ten years to mourn the blunder
   Which beggared them. Ten more to muse on plunder.

And half of ten to mass sufficient armies
T'avenge defeat. Oh tell me where the harm lies?

7 OCTOBER, 1940

One does not have to worry if we die:
Whoever dies, One does not have to bother
Because inside Her there is still another
And, that one wasted too, She yet replies
'Nothing can tire out Nature—here's another!'
    Fecundity par excellence is here,
    Lying in labour even on the bier.

Maternity's the holiest thing on earth
(No man who's prudent as well as wise
Concerns himself with what is in the skies);
Drain-deep below the slums another birth
    Sets angels singing—the other noise you hear
    May be the Warning, may be the All Clear.

Comfort ye My people! These reflections
Should help them die politely who must die,
And reconcile those left behind, who sigh
For loss of children or some near connections—
    Reflect! There is no need for grief nor gloom,
    Nature has ever another in Her womb.

Teeming and steaming hordes who helter-skelter
Stampede the city streets, to herd together
Angry and scared, in dark, in wintry weather—
Above ground still? Fear not, there's one deep shelter
    Open alike in Free and Fascist State,
    Vast, private, silent and inviolate.

BLACK-OUT

Night comes now
Without the artistry of hesitation, the surprising
Last minute turn-aside into a modulation,
Without the rising
Final assertion of promise before the fall.

Darkness now
Comes by routine of cardboard shutter, rattle of curtain,
Comes like a sentence everyone's learnt to utter,
Undoubted and certain,
Too stupid to interest anyone at all.

NOTES ON LIFE AT HOME, FEBRUARY, 1942

What sounds fetched from far the wind carries tonight,
Do you hear them? Out where the sheep are
Huddled on wintry hill this cold night,
Under the lea of the hill folded;
There on the hard earth the wind goes
Massively over them, burdened with all that has colded
A thousand hearts, emptied a million hearts,
Slain twice and thrice a million. Over it blows
And like a flood pours into the house, under the doors,
Rushing like blood out of the dying veins, over the living it pours
And so, like a cunningly-channelled flood, empties away, departs
Leaving us dirtied with litter of not our own casualties,
    not our own hearts.

THE NATURE OF THE MOMENT

Bright bar of sun on water, striking across my ceiling,
turning like spiralled rod of glass on a French clock, or silver
hurry of mercury poured from the dentist's bottle.

And day is fine. Who wakens after a night
cold as stone and dark and heavy as stone,
rises a shrunken Lazarus, mummied by cold and death,
to see a bright spear hurled across the room,
still quivering from the cast, dazzling over his head—

Who sees this, on a winter morning of war, and does not tremble
with the same unchosen joy as the sun and the water?

TEACHING TO SHOOT

When we were first together as lover and beloved
We had nothing to learn; together we improved
On all the world's wide learning, and bettered it, and loved.

Now, you stand on the summer lawn and I am to show you
First how to raise the gun to shoulder, bow head, stare quickly,
    and fire.
Then how to struggle with the clumsy bolt, withdraw, return,
    and again fire.

As the evening darkens, even this summer evening, and the trees
Bend down under the night-wind and the leaves rush in a flaming
    fire,
I am to show you how to bend your body, take step lightly—
    and I hold your arm
(Thin and sleek, and cool as a willow-wand fresh in my hand),
And in your hand you clasp fervently this dirty lump, this grenade.

This thing you hold as you once held my hand is ready to kill.
We intend it to finish those who would finish us—we who are
    not ill,
Are not old, are not mad; we who have been young and who still
Have reason to live, knowing that all is not told.

In your hand you hold iron, and iron is too old;
And steel, which breaks and shatters and is cold;
And our hands are together as always, and know well what they hold.

READING MY OWN WORKS

I hear my own voice, over the desert of days,
Across the sandy stretch of the war I see my own words;
And I had almost forgotten that once I could speak.

You who read words when you want them,
Who turn on the tap of a book, who pour a poem
Half-emptied down drain—It is urgent you understand
How bounteous the words looked, how coolly the mirage
Flowed over sand.

In those far mornings, when the cold winter lay
palely outside and the sky was black,
there came early that lonely herald of day,
the shepherd; walking stiffly back
from hut and field on the upland height
where snow, that cruel winter, hid the ground
and ewes were lambing, forth in the frigid night
bringing frail young ones. And the road would sound
grunting under his tread as the snow packed.
Dark, dark hung the massive sky
and his poor, winking lantern lacked
power to drive off the darkness. He went by
in a frosted gleam for a moment, and that was all.

Up on the hill the darkness was clear as glass
and there was no blur of silence. The lambs calling,
the ewes with narrow feet piercing to grass
under the snow, and the light flakes falling, falling,
made a tune clear to his ear, this old man moving
careful to rhythm of work and music and season.
Down in the village where callous of life and loving
the thatch-rooves huddled, there the winter of reason
bit at his heels, blacked out his vision, and shut
music from ears. The old man past my window
walked, and the steep way to home from hut
was the way from birth to the grave—so slow
he passed, with the dark on his shoulders like a pall.

NEW PAULUS SILENTIARIUS

I

Paulus Silentiarius, asserting that the fire
No longer burned within him, told his mistress,
'I am dying of cold.'

In these days we know other flames beside desire
But the most fearful still, of private distress,
Is life growing cold.

He said that the altar flames, having devoured the sacrifice,
Would slacken, grow grey and die for lack of fuel,
Leaving the altar cold:

His image here is no more than a lover's device
Reproving a mistress transiently cruel,
But I am dying of cold.

II

I show you to the Sun; as if you were a burning-glass
He throws the weight of his light against you
And you direct it to consume me.
I show you to the shadows, holding you out to the night,
Willing to consign you to the Shades, but the river
Dark and stilly-flowing receives you, wears
You bright as the moon set silver on its deathly water—
What fool, my desperate heart, would call that stream Lethe?

SALTHOUSE, NEW YEAR'S EVE

The cold stands tall as a tower to the stone-white moon,
It rises from darkness out of the prostrate sea;
And dead the shore sleeps, now as the slow earth turns
From pretence of a past year to pretence of new.

How dare we stand alone on this empty shore
From which all life was drained with the waning year,
We who believe in Time, in passing and coming?
We do not dare; we stand because we must.

And yet, look down at the sea; her subtile body
Rears tall and cold towards the white-faced moon;
And within her cold black breast a heart-beat stirs,
And throughout this cold last night she breathes and sleeps.

So stand we here, and the round earth heels over,
Bearing the living sea, leaving the moon;
Heavy with night and winter, the earth turns over,
Her children borne safe on her breast towards the sun.

The white tread of the poet like snow footprints on dark earth
Traces a pattern hard to follow, further than sight
Can see or wit give meaning to.
The long landscape of the country known
To many tourists stretches into night
And many tourists vanish with the light.

One child perhaps may stand behind, a solitary,
Small on the flat eternity of earth,
Following white footprints on and on and on
Until at last he sees the distant figure
And, looking back over the journey done,
Perceives a patterned way clear drawn by two.

IMPRESSION OF THOUGHT

Over my mind a tilted cup spilled
A spinning arc of water, spread
Into a cape for shoulders burdened
Till then with too much. The cup ran water
Clear into swift geometrical design
And nothing gaped below to hold it, nor filled
To hold forever till it stank and died.
Lively, strict, fast-glancing past my eye
Thought flashed like water, vanished, and was mine.

IN DREAMS, IN VISION OF THE NIGHT

Through the dark caverns of under-sea,
Through corridors dusky with gold and the old
Black bones of ships, the wooden ribs,
To ivory battlements built of whale
And filigree fish-bones; through the places
Out to the streets and lanes, in strange
Strangled darkness deep and cold,
There walk the sailors who drowned long since.
The tall and the little; the dark-skinned, delicate
Flowers of warm lands; and ebony men;
All, with our own, all turned to the same
Compatriot colour of skeleton bone.
Treasure and plunder and loot lie under
Dense miles of glass-green darkness; there
Brittle feet rattle on round guinea-cobbles
And all is common, not rare nor fair.
What do they say, the bones among bones?
What do they say, blind bones in the darkness?
That nothing is lovely without the light—
That nothing is lovely without the light.

The daggers dreamed on nights alone,
The starving outcry from cold river
Heard in the long midnight of summer,
The wraith that cannot speak or move
And has no home but haunts our love;
These, the unspeculative ghosts,
Symbols of ignorance and will,
These crowd upon us to make known
The way out if we want it. Still
The stay-at-home may sail far coasts
While Much-Afraid sits safe and reads
Strange stories of her wild and undone deeds.

ROUSSEAU'S PICTURE: 'THE FOREST'

Among the tall impossible trees
She walks in her long gown, in her velvet sleeves,
And on high branches grow the fern-frond leaves:
She clasps her heart, startling at what she sees
Out here, beyond the forest, where we stand,

But from the invisible sunrise light
Streams in the painted sky, and summer's day
Is come for ever. She'll for ever stay
There in her fearless world—it was so slight
A threat that she could quiet it with her hand.

Every day perhaps, but surely on sunlit days,
The shadow falls once fair and square on the hour,
And passes again, and is gone until to-morrow.
Remember—through the dawn and evening haze
And at high noon when the bee hangs drunk in the flower—
Remember to note the sundial's punctual sorrow.

DREAM

White Niagara, dark Nigeria,
White on a dark face the eyes and the teeth
Only, vision and voice,
The sight and the word; these white
And the whiteness is noise,
Is brilliance and clatter:
Darkness is all the rest,
The brow and the smooth breast,
Warmth here, and room
In this dusky gloom
For the long luxury of night.
Remote and unwatched, low lies Nigeria.
Brightened by gazing eyes flashes Niagara;
Water murders itself to scatter
Splinters of bright noise to deafen;
From high pours the torrent, underneath,
Wide as this velvet blackamoor heaven,
The dark pool deepens, drawing-in silence:
One is beauty and one is vileness,
Both are eternity, neither gives death.

The honey-pale lioness drowsing in the sun
Is dappled with shadows from flat leaves above her;
While the sharp blades of little shady grasses
Streak her smooth flanks, draw map-lines on her sides.
The flat, transparent surface of her eyes
Lets in the gaze of the sun, and when they close
The earth drowns into darkness. In the pale
Twin wells of her eyes two worlds drown when she covers
Their light with night, and sleeps in her noonday dark.

DREAM LANDSCAPE WITH GIRL

Draw wide the shadows and from the whispered aside
of curtains lean out serene my love and white
to welcome and begin our one enchanted night.

You have long limbs. Your riches bold and grave
outbid the splendour of my life and death
you carry the wealth of Persia light as a rose's breath.

This is the last small room from which the moonlight
looks out with promise. Watch me as I banish
the years remaining and let the promise vanish
and turn to you—Oh watch me as I turn,
for the whole dream is lost if you are not there when I turn!

The long future,
Long as a roll of thunder among the hills,
Long as the line of arched waves coming to shore,
The long future stretches past death and before it;
All except Now is future.
Watching how water stills
After the rain and the wind have passed,
I have seen Now. Watching the drops of rain
Tap on the surface of water, be received, and vanish,
I have seen Now. And in blank darkness,
When the remembered sun fevers blind eyes,
I have seen Now and known it for what it is,
The round drop of time fallen on eternity.

The rich horn blowing of that motor passing
   luxuriously down the summer lane
comes like the scent of thunder over hayfields,
   is a warm cloth laid over aching ear,
comfortable and quieting to despair.

The rich are that to the affrighted or
   to the thin-wrapped, the tired trudging home;
their summer splendour lights, they say, our winter—
   and so they pass and pleasure with them goes,
with the rich horn the red warmth of the rose.

From where we walk and talk to There:
And there is no house, no home, no castle,
But is a falling hovel.
Our destitution is our destination;
Hovel-home, we hobble towards the grave.

Feather in air, silk-shot colours bright;
Curve in its falling, the rainbow tilting;
How beautiful we are in our beginning,
Careless and spendthrift, having no thrift to save.

The hovel's dark on a black night; the air
Being but ice; and all our being ice
Because this has fallen about us:
From the dark air winter has fallen here,
And we have had our spring, and spring is all we have.

Do you ever look over, and see the refugees standing behind the wire?

Call them Displaced Persons, and the image is clearer:
I am about to draw an Image on the wall of our cave.

No need to sketch-in Terror, like a tree grown tall and strident;
no need to have a foreground of Ourselves, this side the wire;
no need, either, to show them innocent or bewildered,
with confusion of flying garments, with round eyes, long hair:
no need for anything but the plain statement in foreground—
A very large assembly, standing still and waiting.

What do the others in our cave say? Bored with it;
They glance, in case there is significance, and reassured, look away

Watch. With my graving flint I scratch more lines:
That tremendous sweeping curve, that is the edge of Time;
they are out beyond it, they are Displaced Persons.
Another curve sweeps round, behind their backs, away—

that is the nearest edge of Eternity; they are outside,
they have their backs to it; they are Displaced Persons.

What do the others in our cave say? Nothing.
Do not disturb them yet. I have more lines to draw.

This time, what? Animals; a frieze of lively creatures
fringing the curve of Earth, to show that here is life;
And only a seagull-pattern of fine ripples behind the other curve,
indicating water, a wide ocean, Eternity:
And in between the standing, staring, waiting rabble,
a Huddle of dead people, the forever-Displaced Persons.

Disturb the others now! Drive them, prod and herd them!
Look—the whole side of our cave is graved with this cartoon.

And I have done what you dreaded: this has a fierce significance—
it brims with potent magic, violent to make you see.
Refugees! Refugees! Driven over the frontier, no permit to go
    further—
This is how we shall all stand, prisoned in the great cage;
behind the wire of death, homeless and staring forever
back into life—and behind us the lovely, eternal sea.

Oh, disturb the others to look and understand!
The lost dead are homeless, stateless for ever more.

Yet, if they would turn, there is no wire between them and the sea—

JOURNEY FROM WINTER

As days become shorter and the cold ghost of the North
leans across from the Pole to strike us, and winter appears in the sky,
it is time to consider our journey. Take down the guides,
the schedules of trains and of sailings, the smart list of 'planes;
and here by the first fire, our comfort and warning, consider:

The ways of coming at truth, attaining creating or re-discovering,
need no special equipment of faith or unfaith;
the amateur party about to set out to-morrow
will follow one route of the three; but all run together
somewhere in country uncharted, and all reach the end.

There are no true maps of the kingdom; guides have been and returned,
but some will not venture again, while others will shepherd part-way
and still others travel as exiles working a passage home.
The natives are foreign to us and will offer no kindness,
being without interest in strangers and unable to speak our tongue.

They say the first stages are easy; civilised travel
and pleasant companions en route. But once over the frontier
there's nothing to help you except your own wits, and the wish
to reach your objective. Once over the frontier the others
who started out with you scatter, and each one travels alone.

Guide-books agree that the country is full of silence;
no written words to be found, no signposts, no place-names, no roads,
and scarcely a living man met. All you can do
is watch for the flight of birds or study the slant of the stars
or try to decipher the hieroglyphs drawn by sheep on the hills.

You can live on the country, they say, and do better so
than to carry provisions which, under that sky, will rot.
You can travel fast or slow; there is nothing to tell you
how much further you have to journey until you arrive,
how much further before you reach—

Reach what? I do not know.
All I know is the blight of the North wind, the carrion
patience of winter hanging up there in the sky,
and the blow that is aimed from the Pole, that is aimed to destroy us.
These things, and the date of starting, are all I know.

OF DEATH AND JUDGEMENT

When the dread Judge upraises himself on his elbow
and in expectance we wait while the bells of Old Bailey dictate
the strict sentence; we do not catch the exact
wording for the fact of his stammer cuts head off, or tail,
or the heart, or at least some part from his slow-
spoken sentence. In hammer-blow, dead, the wigged head
from side to side drums like the thump of bells
in cloisters of head, and aye goes wig-wag as they said.

So you cry aloud, you die aloud, Love; you cry
to the Judge in his shroud diminished and dry,
and loud out they fly, the pigeons and doves to the sky!
And back into marble he drops and is packed
flat again, and the whole fabric is cracked
by the whack of the flapped wings, and loud overhead
as we wake the trumpets of sunrise are red.

NOTES FROM A DIARY

The suave symbols, the words
seen twice, thrice, then not again;
a visit dreamed and next day the comer;
a tree vast and dark on the downs and the long shudder
of recollection, almost:
the keen, pitiful tears sharply starting from pain
for what? A ghost.

These are the symbols, heralds of sharp tempest
of spirit, of Holy Ghost, of the storm in the bone;
can these bones live?

From their drouth the white bones move;
drily they move in the sun, aridly love,
finally weep and in helpless passion become man.

Faith is the long stillness before the tempest blows;
Faith loafs on the quayside catching
nothing, loafing and watching
all through the sultry day till the red storm-cone shows.

Does the lark build its nest on the ground? you asked,
Yes, I said, right on the ground,
As low as it can get and under
A tuft, maybe, or couched in a little hollow.
And is the lark that bird that flies way up, almost gone,
Almost out of sight? you asked,
And I said, Yes.

A very simple question to answer you asked,
But something sang through the sound
Of that, and Yes. Not asunder
The tune from the texture of music, the follow
Of woodwind on strings, nothing is made alone:
Is the bird the ground and the sky, you asked,
And I said, Yes.

On this day
If you called me I would come:
With the wind crying so no heart is dumb,
No feet reluctant now to tread your way.

And in such weather
If you will send for me, if you will send—
I will be quick, will hurry to make an end,
Taking as map to you this blown dove's feather.

I walked through a wood:
I remember, I walked through a silent wood
Where steadfast and tall the trees stood
And pigeons motionless upon their boughs
Never moved, never stirred
So much as to shed one grey breast-feather;
Nor does that wood harbour any other breed of bird.

There to stay would be possible:
For a year, for a week, for a day
Or for the whole moment of a lifetime one might stay—
Pacing the shade and dapple of the place, watching the boughs'
Intricate interlace: waiting at last to tell
What solemn word they spell,
Their darkness tracing on the sky's clear light
Creation's single word.

In time ago the men who would be holy
Housed themselves in the desert, beyond reach of life;
There stood at the frontier of eternity and stared
Across to that strange country, waiting to go over.

Now no longer any place is found
Where men may wait in patience, looking across into peace,
But a few still travel slowly over lengthening years
And at the end sit waiting in the desert of great age.

All those who stray in the dusky spaces
Between clear days of delusion and the acid
Moonlight of truth admitted;
All those who are light-hearted, whose dark faces
Flash with bright joy or crease to such soft sorrow,
All those who are aboriginal, or left out, or half-witted;
How do they live, outside the radius
Of either false or true?

In the pretended day's bright spotlight
The faces glitter with smiles; in the other zone
Where men see truth's reflected
Brilliance as all they have, there is no light
Except by grace of a dead moon and hidden sun;
What illuminates the cast-outs, unredeemed, neglected?
Only a dusky sun, perhaps,
But constant and their own.

The white face of the Moon moved through my dream,
And the old man said, seeing I watched it go,
  'Do you know what it says? Do you know?
Oh God! Oh God! Oh God! it says as it goes.'

And over my heart, and over the man and the dream
And the white-faced Moon drifting through nightmare woes,
  A bitter flood-tide rose,
The same that the Moon drags on through ebb and flow.

The guiltless Ape swings on from branch to branch;
The Spirit where it listeth blows, and shows
Subtile in elements and brilliant in the rose:
Only Man, the hybrid monster, makes the quaking forest blanch.

The silence develops after:
First, spiders swinging from the rafter
And the uncomfortable cry of the weathercock
And the wind's knucklebones on the lock.
Next, a dry, quick scutter
Of mice in the wainscot; a birdwing flutter,
Brittle as sticks, in the chimney—and notice the dangle,
Greasy and frozen, the white shroud on the candle.
At a long last comes silence; following after
The retreating laughter
Of wind, and the weathercock's wail.
Silence is offered you. Now the frail
Tilted vessel takes that velvet wine,
Fills with the garnet blood of poured-out time.
Silence is in the house now, and does not flow over:
Quietness, the gentle wine, pours out for its lover
Brimful, the goblet of heart and house
Filling at last, stilling weathercock, wind and mouse.

Silence lengthens, too, the white candleshroud,
And lays hand at last on heart: 'Hush, heart—too loud—'

I stared through the opening, into the narrow dark of the room;
'Dear child,' I said, 'How do you do? Are you safe in here?'

The child raised its head and moved, scarcely seen in the gloom;
'Are you not cold?' I asked, 'Lonely? Are you not in fear?'

In my dream I rolled back the stone, I rolled it away from the tomb;
'Come!' I cried, 'Oh wake—rise—come forth, my dear!'

Like the dearest child, the weakling, hardest to wean and rear,
My soul inhabits this house, wandering silent from room to room,
And when I call her comes only shyly near.
Sometimes all day she sits moping until late evening gloom
Fills my tall house and the others grow tired and prepare for bed;
Then if I call her, then she will answer me gently, and lift her head.

.

Watch the round drop fall from the tap;
There, on a puddle of water held in the trough,
It forms a shell-shape, fluted and carved
Purely as moulding on ceiling or wall,
Precise as the fossil earth-found or cockle on shore.

The recurrent pattern of water drawn on the world
Is image of all that we knew, all rediscovered
After long search, the word, the secret, the way:
Round as a world the drop falls,
Traces the word, and is gone.

The most persuasive argument is there,
In the cool and reasonable air;
That which is clear, translucent, that which flows
Soft as a river, telling as it goes
Of the tall hills it sprang from, of the sea
To which it travels, of the invisible sea.

And like some inland creatures, we who dwell
Beside the flowing air, hearing it tell
Of unknown past and future, of its birth
Far from us, of its bourne beyond the earth,
Accept the strange persuasion, wonderingly
Move on ourselves towards the invisible sea.

Whether the lost thing found, the exile reaching coast
Late and at last, a wide ocean crossed
And foothold on soil once more:
Which, soul does not know for sure, but feels
Sometimes this, and sometimes as if she were still
Alien, a stateless creature, one without knowledge of home:
Until, on an evening perhaps, when the west wind steals
Like the ghost of summers past over the greying hill,
Suddenly soul awakes, and knows she has come
To the place that's her own.

And now in welcome the sky
Lights star after star on high; and the world sails on,
Stately, a ship into darkness going, tall on the seas
Of calm and eternal night;
And all on board her are safe, and bound for home.

IN THE BEGINNING

Lucifer! Lucifer!
As he fell the last swerve of his foot
Set the earth spinning around the solemn sun.

The sun in judgement sitting:
Lucifer hangs
Cold as a hawk in the blazing sky:

Death like a shadow is on him;
In wax and in wane
He follows his sentence out:

Sometimes at night his pale, extinguished form
Wears light again:
Lucifer, son of the midnight morning!

Only a dead planet catching the light of the sun —
Out in the dark
A son of God hangs.

Lucifer! Lucifer!
Between life and death the world travels,
Spun by a stroke of his foot round the solemn sun:

The cuckoo sang and away the wall echoed his song,
Patiently called again and again, the day long;
And punctual echo answered with his word
Flung back to him, until night stilled the bird.

But with the stars alight and darkness not deep
This clement night of spring, he waking from sleep
Calls drowsily; and now no cry from thence
Replies, but his sound drowns in the deep silence.

The skull leaned forward and said 'Kiss me!'
Thrusting forward, 'Kiss me!' it cried;
Asking to feel again what it had lost
And lain forgetting, almost, since it died—
The pain and the glory.

Newly uncovered, the skull moved blindly:
In brittle obedience the skeleton stirred;
But who would hear and hearing who would come
To love the dumb, the lipless mouth whose word
Cried so untimely?

A MOMENT OF TIME

I have wept with you, loved you; I
have walked beside you through the dark dew
under the deep fall of sky;
and in that earliest hour before dawn we have loved, put by
the coming light with the black night passed—
known only that hour and the hour we shall die.

Now in the world none but I
stare at you so with the round-eyed, the woe
of the fool's eye;
no one alive so far lost, so ruined, so certain to die.
I love you, lost in a ghost of your love;
nor can weep, but swing here like a leaf shrunken and dry.

    I saw my shadow on the wall
    And recognised a shape;
    I am well-grown and standing tall,
    Straight-limbed, small-headed, not too strong;
    So many years, much history proud and long,
    Have laboured on me to conceal the Ape.

    But on the wall, squat and thick-set and still,
    He stood there faceless, innocent of word;
    As if he had returned, meaning no ill
    But anxious to establish some old claim:
    I had forgotten his right name
    And called him simply 'Lord.'

ON LAYING DOWN MY PEN

There stands the shadow with a pistol to its head—
Now, as I sit back listening to the fire
Flaring its life away: now, staring at the page
Made ugly as a battlefield by my defeats,
By tries, erasures, jugglings and deceits,
Evasions, desperate sorties, all the savage
Litter of strife: now I can see the cold
Tall shadow rise, and see the thin hand hold—
Oh quiet, Oh comely black!—the pistol pregnant
With all mandkind's salvation. Now at the soundless sound
I see that shadow fall, blossomed with mortal wound,
And hear the dead bell tolling Now! Now! Now!

What proud despair is here thus crowned, thus regnant,
That here allows me leave to die, to live?
I am all body now, cool heart and thoughtless brow;
This is the liberty he came to give.
Freed from my soul, and clay from feet to head,
I sit at ease before the dying fire.

This early morning I saw the Moon—
Was it this morning? or yesterday? or before? I do not remember:
Only that I saw the Moon and thought, 'I shall remember
For ever that I have seen her so.' So long is for ever, so soon
The moment in time I know that I do not remember.

I remember the story of a poet long ago
Who, for offence against the masters then,
Was treated, was barbarously mistreated,
Was—It chokes my heart to remember him.
He was blinded and his tongue torn out,
Both his hands severed, and he was let go.
He lived for years and years and endless years,
Beggared and maimed and silenced and in the dark.
What was his offence? Perhaps none. It was forgotten
Before one-half the maiming had been done.

But I remember him now, almost every day,
Stumbling over my silent, lightless way.

ON A WINTER JOURNEY

On this very cold evening,
When the black horse stands stiffly under a tall black tree
And the wind whitens the lane mud and pales the grass in the meadows,
On this evening I met a strange funeral in the darkening cold.

Ahead of me down the lane went a slow procession:
A tractor drawing a tumbril and a dead calf laid on the cart;
New-born, new-dead, it lay sleek on rough sacking,
And following close, head lowered and white flanks shining,
The cow walked in heaviness and majesty of grief.

After them came the two black-habited mourners,
Two shadows to balance the dazzling white;
Two foreboders, two buriers, two demons, two masters—
In the darkening evening Hodge and his son followed the dead.

But beautiful beautiful the sorrow and majesty and whiteness,
And the dead creature so still, so sleekly lying!
Something long known, never questioned, in meekness accepted,
The slow procession down a darkening lane
Of the dead and the mother, and the silent black masters.

'There were times long ago,' she said,
'Do you know—
If you take a bird's feather, even from a bird that's dead,
And if you blow, even lightly, even so—'
And she sighed, so—
'It will fly, it will fly—
And so it was when I was young,' she said.

'Everyone has something to know,' I said,
'But to show
So little—and now that all my time has fled
I scarcely know one line, nor have to show
Even a feather, to show
That once I set a bird to fly, to fly—
And yet it seemed I did,' I said.

POEM FOR THE PASSING OF POETRY

Praise God for the sheep on the tall green hill,
And for the shadows passing over the grass where they walk;
Praise God for the spear-heads of weeds in the river,
And for the heart-shapes they make when the flow changes;
Praise God for the flower of the rose and its cruel stalk,
For the moonlight pallor of spring as it dies forever,
For the careless wind that wakens and then estranges—
Praise God for the things I saw when I walked on the hill.

AUTOBIOGRAPHICAL

Lie down on a battlefield, or make love to the tune of *Greensleeves?*
I could each, my Love, die or give life; because
The day is not only the dove in a morning waking
But noon at white stare of light, and evening when bats replacing
The twilight swallows in flight, precede themselves the owls
Who cry 'Woe, woe,' and shriek ' "Tis he! Tis he!",
Outside our blank uncurtained window.

Since childhood, choice has been my worst besetter;
Which of two colours? Which of two odours? Which of two favours?
Which of two saviours?
Should I grow up promoter or begetter? Should I leap to the barricades,
Shout 'Liberty!' and die? Or live obscurely, in humility,
And scale the highest heights none but the blind can see,
The blind who have met their Lord and been restored to see.

Lie down on a battlefield, make love to a tune, or make the tune?
Or live—and watch the landscape of life change, as if I saw
The colours on a distant planet change, and learned its seasons so,
And learned no more of it than that the thing was so.

Where there is something underneath the sweetness,
Under the flower, beneath the bright green grass,
Buried in earth, sullen and deep and lightless,
The bulb stays, couched in the long roots of the grass.

There do I love you finally and for ever;
Not sweet-renouncing, not unminding colour,
But knowing us even at root beloved and lover—
And true, even in the darkness beneath the colour.

The sea-crab swings its cabriolet body
Slung on slings of arched legs, and hurries,
Making good time over foundering tracks
Between rocks to the sea, to the sea.

What matter if rocks are our pebbles, its ocean
Our scooped hole in sand, by a miracle filled
With glittering teaspoons of water?

Know that the crab-soul
Sitting somewhere concealed in that odd vehicular wonder
Stares out like a girl from a curtained window,
And the little clumsy travelling carriage is taking
Immortal Incognita to the beautiful waiting sea.

HOPE OF POETRY

Sometimes in the bleakest days of winter, after the turn of the year,
When the knout of the north wind flays us and the earth is black and bare,
You may see the unbelievable, tender green of a plant
There risen from the stripped and anguished earth, there shining like a flame . . .
So is it with my hope, risen from just such a death-bed winter,
And I am touched to tears by the tender green of my hope,
Standing as I do in the reach of the falling knout,
Stroke after stroke, and the black-uniformed winter still there—
Still with the knout in its swollen empurpled hand.

Man, beaten to iron-hard earth and the strokes still falling,
Lie low as you need, but fear nothing. The little green flame still presses
Out from the hard ground, and even the jack-boot treading
Cannot quench this tongue of bright fire from the heart of the world.

Into this brief and angry place
The sun shone his bell
Ringing the waking
Skies with morning, and the walls of the cell
Opened to fields and his sleep-washed face
Felt air again, all air for the taking:
Because the sun's bell rang for his death
And the furious moment had gone, had gone like a breath—

For all that takes place under this dome of the sky:
For the gentle, exhausted deer;
For the bitter cry,
The desperate last cry of the hare;
For the small cubs flung for hounds to tear;
For the badger, the otter, the fox—for all here
Hunted and driven over their own ground, the land
That is theirs, so small a portion of it under the sky:
For this and for these who now will dare
Speak any word of excuse or call mercy with a prayer?

Heavy with guilt and the weight of woe,
Standing waist-deep already in the rising flood,
We keep our eyes closed, our minds blank, not to know
What black deed we do. And may we so
Win some kind of forgiveness, some shabby salvation
Among those others who knew not what they did?
They too spilled royal blood, slew what should wander free,
Innocent and careless, clad in grace of divinity;
And 'Truly—' they said, looking on him when they had done,
'Truly this was the Son of God!' But they had done what they had done.

And the flood rises and the flood rises and the blood flows and the blood flows;
And we turn on each other, father on son and brother on brother;
And the flood rises and the blood flows—
And carelessly, every summer, blooms and burns and falls the rose.

Lead, somehow, our slow minds to thy truth,
In this swift time that we pass between life and life;
Or we shall lose all, and for the little gain
Of being untroubled in our quick passing-through.

The gourd grew and was a shade, and died and was nothing:
Jonah, excoriated by the wind and the sun,
Complained; said he did well to complain, but God
Replied only that He had mercy for men and beasts as well.

The truth startles for a moment, and is gone again;
Flash of a bright eye in the thicket seen
And vanished in the moving flickering green
Of leaves and grass and shadows: but only so truth shows.

Only so truth is seen: for a moment's moment as we go
Like thistledown on the wind, between life and life.

VARIATIONS ON A THEME

'Forgive the Sleeping Man'

I
1934

Fallen on grass, the drought grass pale and brittle,
With such wide stretch of arid meadow
Beyond his round head, slack feet and around him;
Sleeping here he seems strayed, uncared-for, little—
Mean in his mean clothes, and I in my mean clothes watching,
And in the sun. Forgive the sleeping man:
Not careless, not at ease, not free in air,
Not living. Mortally sick instead, and the sickness catching.

Kill him we must. Not rouse. Already dead and swaddled
In cerements that already stink to heaven
He is dead, is dead.
By falling to sleep there unwarily he saddled
Himself with the weight of death and the weight is pressing—
Forgive the sleeping man, the dead man!
Ask grace for deed done. More easily than the murdered
Murderers find it—But from whence comes blessing?

II
1936

God, awake always,
Forgive the sleeping man.
Man has not many days, and here in sunlight
Lies he sleeping, low down on the earth lying;
Lips set and solemn, head laid down as though the dying
Had been quite easy, and his gentle hair
Compassionately spread in wing-shape over brow.

Those who have not known sleep
Might well think waking fine.
This man lay down to weep and fell instead
Into the quietness of Man's deep despair;
Lies now in the silence of the last word said.
Nothing is strange, or sorrowful, or new—
Quietly he sleeps, and does not even dream.

III
1943

Oh the man that sleeps yet
Holds under his closed eyelids
The darkening, the fading ashes
Of that fire we remember;
Still we discern the fire,
The sharp tongues of a summer
Whose brief, immediate radiance
Sleeps beneath his eyelids.

IV
1948

The man who sleeps, whose soul has fled,
Is man-alone, whether he sleeps in bed
Or in the grave; let spirit but begone
And back comes innocence. With all his sinning done,
Man lies here tranquil now the God has fled.

V
1950

The man who drowns, see how he rests his head!
I saw him once, saw him laid on the water dead;
And in the flowing stems of his meek hair,
In the arched throat, the swaying of his lightly pillowed head,
I saw all loveliness of sleep, and all care banished.

Trouble of thought, fevers, the spinning words,
Torment of right and wrong, of lost and found,
Loud daylight cries, the muffled night-winged birds,
Splinters of sky, masterful earth: when he forsook the ground
All these were conquered, and he so could lie
Gently upon the rocking water and untroubled die.

VI
1957
(Rousseau's picture: 'The Sleeping Gypsy')

Who cried, long years ago, 'Forgive the sleeping man'?
And now, who here sleeps, closed within the span
Of emptiness and light? Here lies the born,
And nothing in the landscape or the morning
Predicates death. Here woman newly made
Sleeps safely still, in opened light;
And here the lion Sun can stand beside her
Unthwarted yet by body's cry for shade.
Here, tidy, side by side, her feet
Which never yet trod earth; her hands are still,
And she alone in all the empty land.

Forgive the sleepers, Lord! Thou didst so make them.
Receive them when they wake and Oh! indulgently awake them.

VALENTINE ACKLAND
1906—1968

A lyrical disposition, a chess-playing mind, an implacable regard for truth—these are the constants in Valentine Ackland's poetry as they were in her character. It was a perilous compound, for truth is an explosive and the chess-playing mind excelled in finding reasons to despair. She was impersonally ambitious; she wanted recognition for her poems, not for herself.

> Let me young grow up—
> They fill the nest up—
> There's no room for more eggs—
> They fill the nest up.
>
> Let my birds fly—
> Either move or die—
> They must soon be gone—
>   Let them out to fly.
>
> Unless they soon go
>   No one will know
> What strong wings they have—
>   Unless they soon go.

This early poem held good throughout her life. The vitality and instantaneity of her poems were recognised by Edmund Wilson, and between the mid-Thirties and mid-Forties many were published in *The New Republic*, others in *New Masses* and *The New Yorker*. She had always been a reader of contemporary poetry, not less so after the emergence of the post-war poetry, which dated hers. Grieving for the non-recognition of her later poems, she recognised herself as a poet, and wrote on, faithful to a life-long ambition to write the kind of poetry which would convey truth and the moment with plain-dealing integrity.

www.ingramcontent.com/pod-product-compliance
Lightning Source LLC
Chambersburg PA
CBHW031429290426
44110CB00011B/589